As an example of how these prefixes are used, let us examine the taxonomy of the Gila Monster lizard which is a present day inhabitant of Arizona:

Kingdom — Metazoa
    Phylum — Chordata
        Class — Reptilia
        Subclass — Diapsida
        Infraclass — Lepidosauromorpha
            Superorder — Lepidosauria
            Cohort — (not applicable)
        Order — Squamata
        Suborder — Lacertilia
        Infraorder — Diploglossa
            Superfamily — Varanoidea
            Family — Helodermatidae
                Genus — *Heloderma*
                species — *Heloderma suspectum*

In the pages that follow, all the animals described are of the Kingdom Metazoa, Phylum Chordata, and Class Reptilia.

TURTLES

Subclass Testudinata
Order Chelonia
Suborder Cryptodira
Superfamily Baenoidea

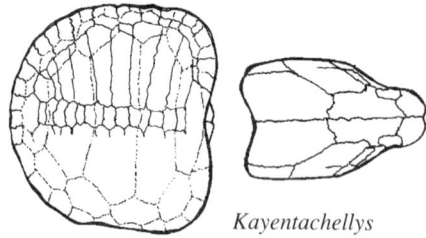

Kayentachellys

Four taxa of Mesozoic turtles have been found in Arizona. All of them are members of the Superorder Cryptodira (turtles that retract their heads by folding cervical (neck) vertebrae in an s-shape, in the vertical plane).

The earliest turtle known in Arizona is *Kayentachellys aprix* from the Early Jurassic Kayenta Formation in northern Arizona. This turtle is considered the earliest known Cryptodire. This turtle could not retract its head but it had the precursor characteristics, in the neck and skull, necessary to permit the evolution of this kind of movement.

Other Mesozoic turtles found in Arizona include: the sea turtle *Dematochelys lowi* from Mancos Shale of Black Mesa, and the soft-shelled turtles *Trionyx sp.* and *Plastomenus sp.* from the Fort Crittenden Formation in the Santa Rita Mountains.

ARIZONA DINOSAURS: AN INTRODUCTION

The reptiles that evolved during the Mesozoic Era — also referred to as the Age of Reptiles — are the focus of this Field Guide. It was during this time that giant dinosaurs roamed the earth, the first mammals evolved, and the first birds flew. The emphasis of this guide is the more prominent Mesozoic reptiles and dinosaurs who lived and roamed in Arizona.

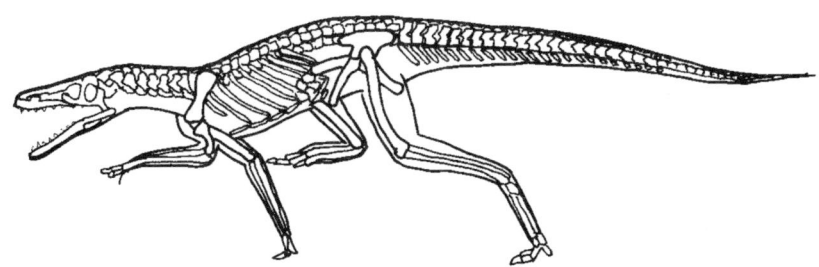

The Mesozoic Era began 245 million years ago (mya) and ended 66 mya. It is divided into three periods: Triassic Period (245—208 mya), Jurassic Period (208—144 mya), and Cretaceous Period (144—66 mya).

TAXONOMY AND SYSTEMATICS

A method has been developed by biologists called the Linnaean system. This system classifies all living things and shows their genetic relationships to each other. In the Linnaean system, there are five kingdoms: Monera (bacteria), Fungi (mushrooms), Protista (protozoa and algae), Metazoa (animals), and Metaphyta (plants).

Each kingdom is subdivided into phylum. These subdivisions are further divided into class, then order, family, and genus until all genetic relationships are established. The smallest subdivision of a kingdom is the species that actually represents a specific type of animal or plant.

Reptile taxonomy does not always fit the basic Linnaean system. In paleontology, researchers have found that a given taxonomic term does not adequately describe the hierarchical arrangement of animal groups. Additionally, the definition for the term for the next level up or the next level down is too broad or too narrow.

Scientists describe additional subdivisions with the terms super, sub, cohort, and infra. When applicable, super, cohort and sub are used to infer that the taxonomy described encompasses more than or less than what the Linnaean definition provides for. The prefix infra describes a subset of a subset.

TURTLES
Jurassic and Cretaceous Periods
Length: up to 1 meter
(up to 3 feet)

Dematochelys

Trionyx

PLESIOSAURS

Subclass Diapsida
Infraclass Lepidosauromorpha
Superorder Sauropterygia
Order Plesiosauria

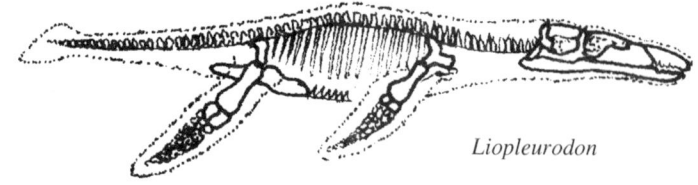

Liopleurodon

Plesiosaurs were marine reptiles of the Jurassic and Cretaceous Periods. These animals were predators and had a propulsion style similar to that of modern sea lions or sea turtles. They had one basic body plan, four flippers and a tail approximately the length of the trunk, which was used as a rudder. There were two variations of this body plan: long neck/small head (elasmosaurs) and short neck/large head (pliosaurs). Fossils representing both body plans have been found in Arizona. For illustration purposes *Liopleurodon* and *Elasmosaurus* are shown.

Plesiosaurs are known from exposures of Mancos Shale, along the edges of Black Mesa, Arizona. All the material found to date has been very fragmentary.

PLESIOSAURS
Cretaceous Period
Length: 3 to 12 meters
(10 to 40 feet)

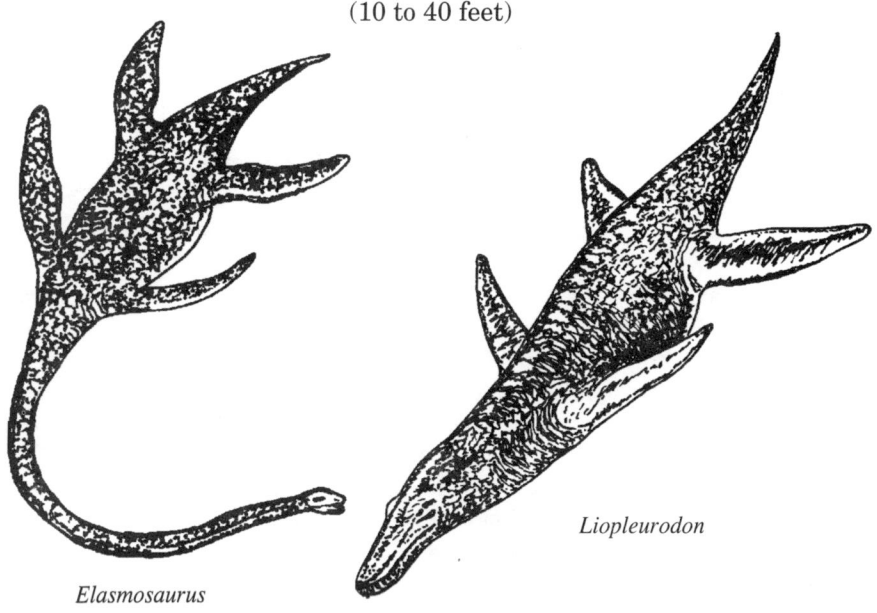

Elasmosaurus

Liopleurodon

POPOSAURS

Subclass Diapsida
Infraclass Archosauromorpha
Superorder Archosauria
Order Thecodontia
Suborder Rauisuchia
Family Poposauridae

Postosuchus·

Three species of this family, *Poposaurus gracilis, Postosuchus kirkpatricki,* and *Chatterjeea elegans,* have been found in Arizona at a number of Triassic-age sites of the Chinle Formation, including the Petrified Forest National Park. They were the largest terrestrial predator of their day.

When *P. kirkpatricki* was described for the first time, three sizes of individuals, a juvenile, a subadult, and a robust adult were described. When other researchers examined the published data, a number of them came to the conclusion that the smallest individual was not a juvenile but an adult of a new species. They named this new animal *Chatterjeea elegans*. The genus name is the latinized form of the name of the researcher, Dr. Sankar Chatterjee who first described *P. kirkpatricki*.

POPOSAURS
Triassic Period
Length: 2 to 5 meters
(6 to 16 feet)

Postosuchus

AETOSAURS

Subclass Diapsida
Infraclass Archosauromorpha
Superorder Archosauria
Order Thecodontia
Suborder Aetosauria
Family Stagonolepididae

There are five species of this family that are found in the Southwest: *Acenasuchas geoffreyi, Desmatosuchas haplocerus, Paratypothorax andressi, Stagonolepis wellsi,* and *Typothorax coccinarum.* This family of Thecodonts is unusual in that they are herbivorous; all other families of Thecodonts are carnivorous. These animals are known only from Upper Triassic formations, including the Chinle Formation in Arizona and New Mexico, the Santa Rosa Formation in New Mexico and the Dockum Group in Texas.

Throughout the Southwest, where Aetosaurs are reported, usually few of these species are found at any given area. In New Mexico, *T. coccinarum* and *S. wellsi* have been identified. In Arizona, *D. haplocersus,* and *S. wellsi* have been found at a number of locations. Interestingly, all five species have been found inside the boundaries of the Petrified Forest National Park.

AETOSAURS
Triassic Period
Length: 2 to 4 Meters
(6 to 13 feet)

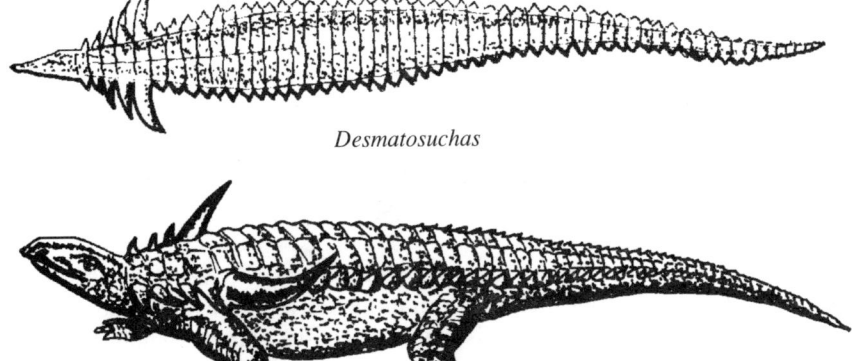

Desmatosuchas

Desmatosuchas

PHYTOSAURS

Subclass Diapsida
Infraclass Archosauromorpha
Superorder Archosauria
Order Thecodontia
Suborder Phytosauria
Family Phytosauridae

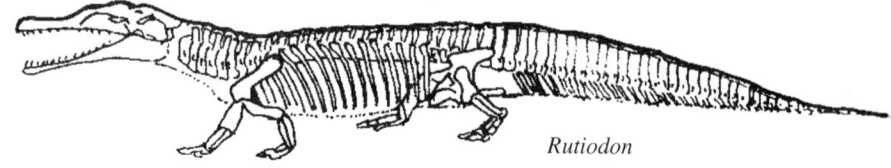

Rutiodon

In Arizona, there are at least nine species of Phytosaurs described in a number of different genera. These animals looked like crocodiles and reached the same size range of modern and historical crocodiles. They are not crocodiles but instead are the predecessors (but not ancestors) of the crocodiles. The position of the nostrils high on the "forehead" is the single best distinguishing feature from crocodiles. Only known from the Late Triassic they became extinct at the end of the Triassic.

Based on the fossil evidence, it is presumed that these animals filled most of the same ecological niches as modern crocodiles.

PHYTOSAURS
Triassic Period
Length: 2 to 12 meters
(6 to 40 feet)

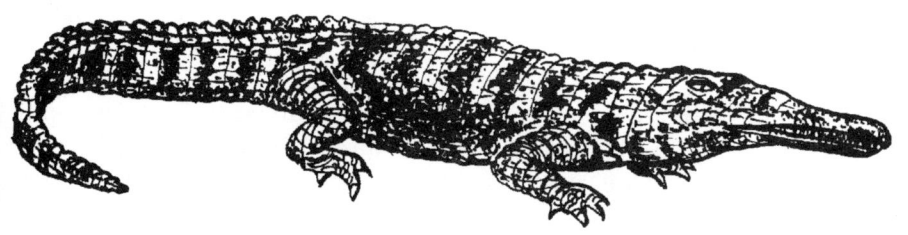

Rutiodon

RHAMPHINION JENKINSI

Subclass Diapsida
Infraclass Archosauromorpha
Superorder Archosauria
Order Pterosauria
Suborder Rhamphorhynchoidea
Family Incertae Sedis

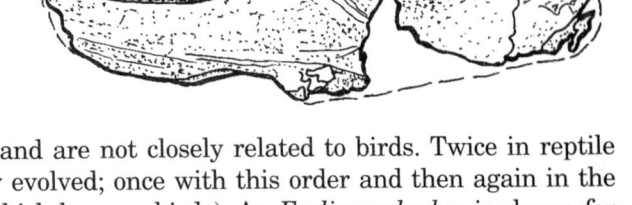

These are reptiles, and are not closely related to birds. Twice in reptile history the ability to fly evolved; once with this order and then again in the theropods (one line of which became birds). An *Eudimorphodon* is shown for illustration purposes.

The Kayenta Formation of Arizona has produced two confirmed Pterosaur fossil finds. The first was fragments of a skull, shown above, and teeth (which this species is based on); the other find was a wing-metacarpal.

In addition, the first reported Pterosaur tracks were found near Four Corners. The tracks were reported in 1957; in 1984 a report stated these tracks were made by a crocodilian; in 1995 other researchers concluded they are actually Pterosaur tracks. All of these findings are still being contested.

RHAMPHINION JENKINSI
(*Eudimorphodon* is shown for illustration purposes)
Jurassic Period
Wing Span: 1 meter
(3.3 feet)

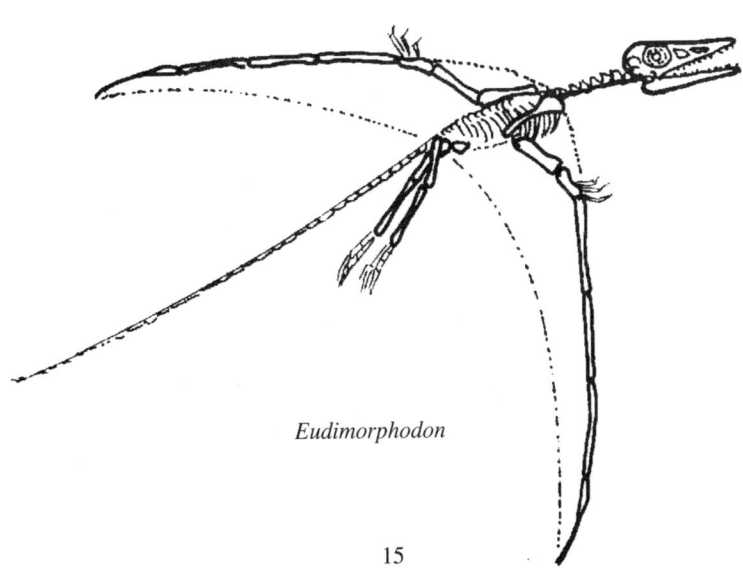

Eudimorphodon

CHINDESAURUS BRYANSMALLI

Subclass Diapsida
Infraclass Archosauromorpha
Superorder Archosauria
Cohort Dinosauria
Order Saurischia
Suborder Therapoda
Family Herrerasauridae

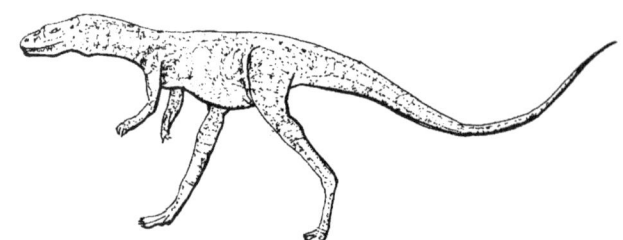

In 1984 paleontologists found bone fragments in the Chinle Formation of the Painted Desert in the Petrified Forest National Park. The discovery was made during the last days of the field season and it was not possible to begin excavation of the find, so the field crew noted the location and returned home.

With the opening of the field season in 1985, a field crew returned to the spot and began excavating. What they ultimately unearthed were the incomplete remains of what was thought to be the oldest dinosaur in the world; that view is no longer held. They nicknamed this fossil "Gerti" after the first cartoon dinosaur.

CHINDESAURUS BRYANSMALLI
Triassic Period
Length: 3.5 meters
(12 feet)

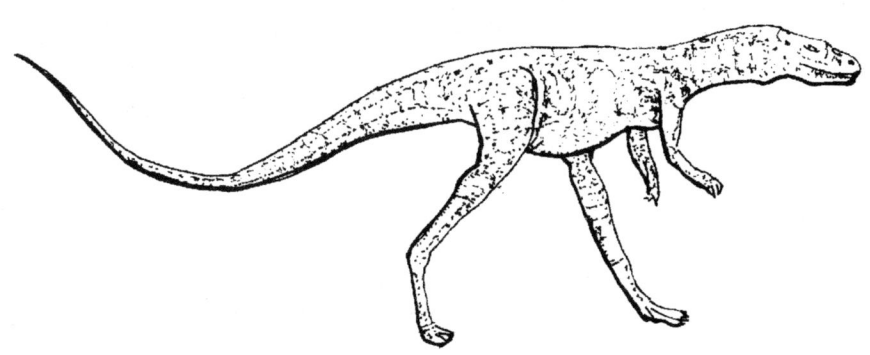

DILOPHOSAURUS WETHERILLI

Subclass Diapsida
Infraclass Archosauromorpha
Superorder Archosauria
Cohort Dinosauria
Order Saurischia
Suborder Theropoda
Infraorder Ceratosauria
Family Podokesauridae

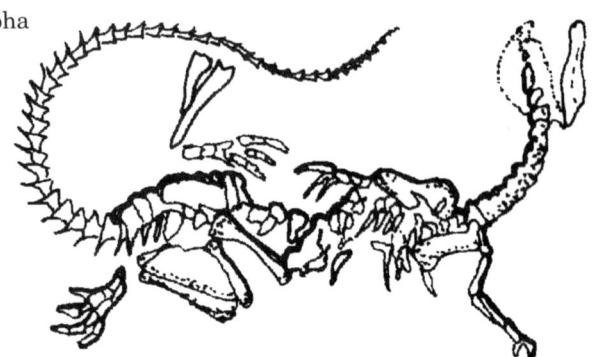

Dilophosaurus wetherilli is a large carnivorous dinosaur known from three subadult individuals found in the Kayenta Formation, north of Cameron, Arizona. The name is derived from the two parallel crests on top of the nose.

There is no paleontological evidence to support presentation of *Dilophosaurus* as a frill-equipped, poison-spitting beast as portrayed in the movie, "Jurassic Park." *Dilophosaurus* does have teeth that evolved for tearing and ripping flesh. However, researchers question if *Dilophosaurus* was an active predator, because like scavengers there is a weakness in the structure of the jaw.

DILOPHOSAURUS WETHERILLI
Jurassic Period
Length: 6 meters
(20 feet)

SYNTARSUS KAYENTAKATAE

Subclass Diapsida
Infraclass Archosauromorpha
Superorder Archosauria
Cohort Dinosauria
Order Saurischia
Suborder Theropoda
Infraorder Ceratosauria
Family Podokesauridae

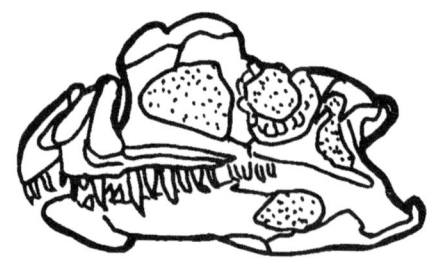

The discovery of *Syntarsus kayentakatae* was reported in 1989. These animals were about the same size as *Coelophysis bauri*. The two animals look very much alike but there are twenty-three morphological differences between them. Some of these differences are the shape of the skull, the number of teeth, and length of forelimbs.

S. kayentakatae was diagnosed based on fourteen partial individuals excavated from the Kayenta Formation in the Little Colorado River Valley. Material representing more individuals was identified in the collections of other museums but all this material is not diagnostic of *S. kayentakatae*. The author of the report admits some of the material may be that of *Segisaurus*.

SYNTARSUS KAYENTAKATAE
Jurassic Period
Length: 2 meters
(Six feet)

TYRANNOSAURIDAE

Subclass Diapsida
Infraclass Archosauromorpha
Superorder Archosauria
Cohort Dinosauria
Order Saurischia
Suborder Theropoda
Infraorder Tetanurae
Family Tyrannosauridae

Knowledge of the Tyrannosaur family in Arizona is based on the finding of more than a dozen teeth by three different teams of researchers over the last fifty years. All the teeth came from the same exposure of Cretaceous Period rocks in the Santa Rita Mountains southeast of Tucson.

The first researcher to find these teeth identified them as *Gorgosaurus libratus*. Later the genus, *Gorgosaurus*, was declared to be a junior synonym of *Albertasaurus*, thereby invalidating the use of the junior name. After examination of subsequent finds, a determination was made that the available data did not support the genus level identification.

For illustration purposes *Albertasaurus* is shown.

TYRANNOSAURIDAE
Cretaceous Period
Length: 8 to 10 meters
(25 to 30 feet)

MASSOSPONDYLUS

Subclass Diapsida
Infraclass Archosauromorpha
Superorder Archosauria
Cohort Dinosauria
Order Saurischia
Suborder Sauropodomorpha
Infraorder Plateosauria
Family Massospondylidae

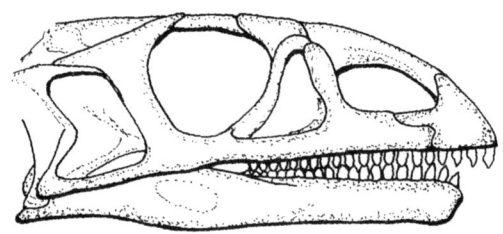

Massospondylus is a Prosauropod dinosaur from the Early Jurassic Epoch. It was found near Rock Head on the Navajo Indian Reservation. This genus was originally known from southern Africa. It grew to a length of about 4 meters. The material found in Arizona consists of a complete skull and lower jaw. Even though the skull is in an excellent state of preservation, a species level identification has not been made.

There is speculation that the material reported as *Ammosaurus* may actually be *Massospondylus* material. A comparison cannot be performed, as the only known skull material of *Ammosaurus* is too badly crushed to be evaluated and no postcranial material of *Massospondylus* has been found in Arizona or elsewhere in North America.

MASSOSPONDYLUS
Jurassic Period
Length: 4 to 6 meters
(12 to 20 feet)

"SONORASAURUS"

Subclass Diapsida
Infraclass Archosauromorpha
Superorder Archosauria
Cohort Dinosauria
Order Saurischia
Suborder Sauropodomorpha
Infraorder Sauropoda
Family Brachiosauridae

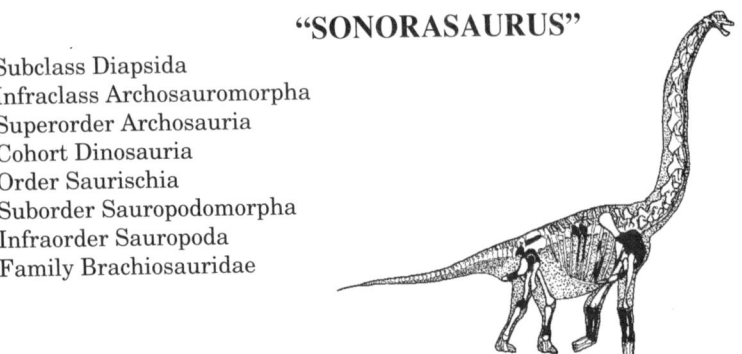

"Sonorasaurus" is a dinosaur currently being excavated from a site in southeastern Arizona. The quotes around the name indicate that this is an informal or field name. A team of researchers from the Arizona Sonora Desert Museum is conducting the excavation of this dinosaur.

Research indicates this animal is a Brachiosauid but at this time not enough diagnostic material has been recovered to make a definite genus or species identification. Comparisons indicate this animal is about 70% the size of the Brachiosaurus on display in the Field Museum in Chicago.

The dinosaur shown on the this page is *Brachiosaurus branci*. The black areas indicate the bones that have been excavated to date. For illustration purposes the dinosaur on the next page is a *Pleuocoelus sp.*

"SONORASAURUS"
Cretaceous Period
Length: 18 to 23 meters
(60 to 74 feet)

SCUTELLOSAURUS LAWLERI

Subclass Diapsida
Infraclass Archosauromorpha
Superorder Archosauria
Cohort Dinosauria
Order Ornithischia
Suborder Stegosauria
Family Scelidosauridae

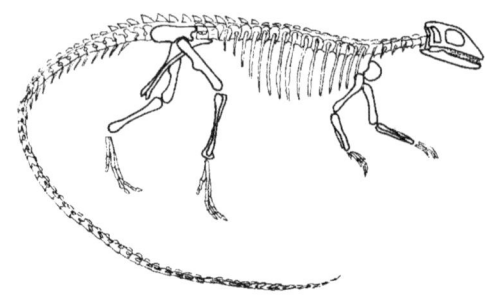

Scutellosaurus lawleri was found in the Kayenta Formation on Ward Terrace. It is the earliest known body fossil of an Ornithischian dinosaur found in Arizona. The first part of its name is derived from the Latin word *scutellum* meaning "little shield." This reference is to the pattern of osteoderms covering the back and sides of this animal.

S. lawleri grew to a length of one to one-and-a-half meters (four to five feet) long. It is postulated that this dinosaur walked in a quadrupedal stance and would probably run in a bipedal manner. The evidence for this is articulation of the front feet, the length of the forelimbs, and the length of the tail. Based upon the observations of bipedal running lizards, a tail of this size would be needed to act as a counterbalance for an animal with this much dermal armor.

SCUTELLOSAURUS LAWLERI
Jurassic Period
Length: 1.5 meters
(4.5 feet)

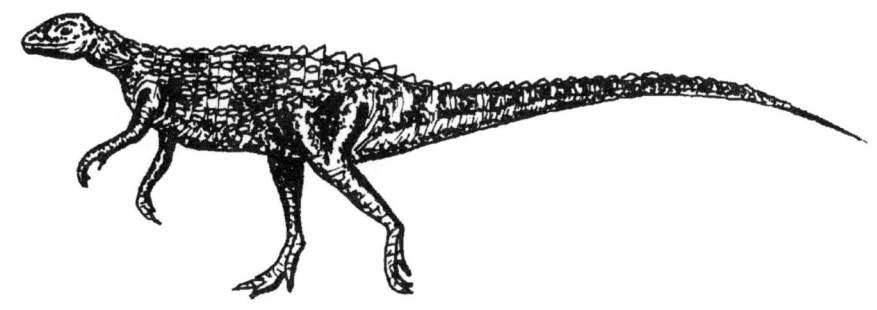

TENONTOSAURUS

Subclass Diapsida
Infraclass Archosauromorpha
Superorder Archosauria
Cohort Dinosauria
Order Ornithopoda
Suborder Ornithischia
Family Hypsilophodontidae

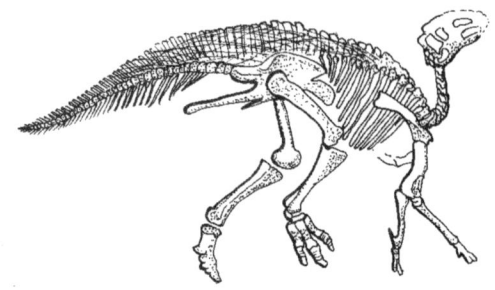

The existence of *Tenontosaurus* in Arizona is known from two femora, one found in the Empire Mountains and one found in the Whetstone Mountains. When these bones were first reported, they were at first identified as an Igaundontid. Later, the identified material was reassigned to this genus.

The family identification shown here is a matter of debate. Since this genus was first described in 1970, researchers have argued whether this genus belongs in the family Hypsilophodontidae, in the family Iguandontidae, or in a new, as of yet, undefined and unnamed family. The conundrum is caused by the fact this genus shares attributes with the primitive family Hypsilophodontidae and the evolved family Iguandontidae. Current information is not sufficient to resolve the question.

TENONTOSAURUS
Cretaceous Period
Length: 1.5 to 7.5 meters
(5 to 25 feet)

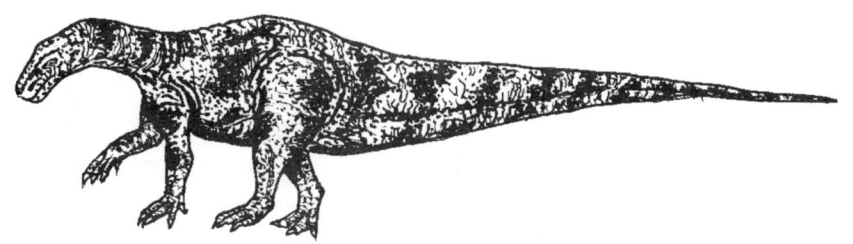

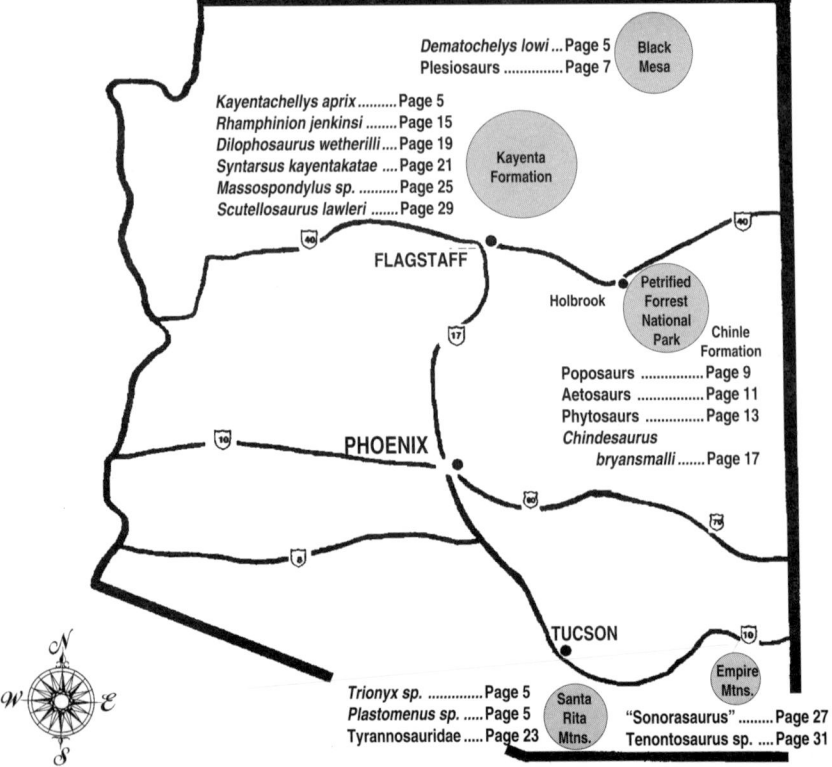